See Beyond Behavior®

A Method for Understanding
and Influencing
Behavior Change

Behavior Environment Health Comparative Analysis

Torri Wright, MA, SPED

Copyright © 2019 Torri Wright, MA, SPED

All rights reserved, including the right to reproduce this book or portions thereof in any form whatsoever.

First Edition, 2017
Second Edition, 2018, 2019

Cover design by Steven Rios

ISBN: 9781720623823

behca.com

Dedication

For the many children, families, and individuals I have had the incredible opportunity to work with over the years, teaching me the language of behavior. To my business partner for his incredible support and encouragement through this process. Thank you for believing in me and this methodology.

Table of Contents

Preface 7

Why BEHCA 9

   A Few Statistics and Thoughts 9

   The Passion Behind It All 12

   Pen-and-Paper Beginnings 15

   Imagining an App 17

   George and Amanda's Family 20

      How BEHCA Could Have Helped 27

Language of Professionals 30

   Breakdown in Communication 33

   Validation of Fear, Frustration, and Stress 35

   How Each of Us Interprets Behavior 44

Self-Reporting 49

Application of Knowledge Gained 59

How Schools Use BEHCA 63

   Writing and Developing IEP (Individual Educational Plan) Goals ... 63

   Creating Solid, Data-Driven BSPs and FAs 66

   Providing Resources for RTI 71

   Communication In All Environments 73

Individual Families and Care Providers 78

   Potential Changes and Impacts of Learning New Things from the Data 86

How to Most Effectively Set Up BEHCA **90**

Conclusion **110**

Glossary of Terms **114**

Questionnaire for Setting Up BEHCA **122**

    Month One Check In 131

    What to Do With Data... 133

Acknowledgements **138**

Preface

This book is an introduction into why BEHCA® (Behavior Environment Health Comparative Analysis) was developed and how BEHCA can be used to decode complex and challenging behavior. Observing environment, health, and daily living encourages us to see beyond the behavior, identifying key influencers, and variables that instigate challenging reactions and interactions.

As human beings, we are complex in how we receive and process information and formulate responses or reactions. Some of us could benefit from tracking, observing, and analyzing these complexities. Fully customized to allow tracking for every individual, BEHCA generates multiple graphs (in the dashboard), showing trends and correlations between the variables over time.

This information allows us to determine and test if the interventions are effective and appropriate. Teaching replacement behavior cannot begin until we understand the behavior, therefore having extended data to review provides this perspective. BEHCA is the tool for this.

BEHCA automatically tracks the natural environment, including daily weather, barometric pressure, humidity, moon phases, and so forth (based on individual location), further expanding the potential for understanding the influence of the environment on our daily living. As a behavior consultant, I have found myself looking in every direction, far and wide, in an attempt to understand the most exact function of a behavior. The level of detail BEHCA is capable of tracking and analyzing allows us to fine-tune and further adjust, until we reach a place of clarity and understanding. This takes a bit of habit building and consistency in inputting information, although well worth the effort.

BEHCA offers an opportunity to learn more about those we support. The process of understanding and investigating behavior can be arduous, elusive, and sometimes seemingly impossible. Our goal is to offer a few strategies, tips, and examples with the intention of making the routine a little easier, as well as to promote a shift in how we, the observers, see challenging behavior and what it communicates.

Why BEHCA

A Few Statistics and Thoughts

In the United States, one out of every five adults have a disability, according to a newer study published by the Center for Disease Control and Prevention. This equates to nearly 20 percent (57 million) of the US population. The most common functional disability type is a mobility limitation — defined as serious difficulty walking or climbing stairs — reported by one in eight adults, followed by disability in thinking and/or memory, independent living, vision, and self-care.

This same research found a higher percentage of individuals with disabilities were generally from the southern states, which speculated that this may be in correlation with the higher rates of chronic diseases, such as heart disease and diabetes. While this is interesting information to know or consider, one might begin to hypothesize why there is a higher rate of chronic illness in the southern regions. Perhaps it is directly related to socioeconomic status, the ability to access proper health care, increased exposure to environmental pollutants, weather -

related influences, less education around nutrition and self-care, or some other factor not considered.

BEHCA can assist in learning more about those correlations. BEHCA may not solve the issue; however, a collection of data is powerful in the way of creating solutions to solving problems. Challenging behavior, disabilities, and human limitations are symptoms of a larger influence on our way of living. Quality of life can always be improved when we recognize the function of a behavior or the influence of an ailment.

With a continued rise in disabilities, challenging behavior has become a common focus in schools, communities, and homes throughout the world. A shift in how we see behavior may be needed before we dive in to collecting data. Behavior is typically most challenging for the people around those expressing the behavior, while in one way the behavior is serving that person (most often as a form of communication or protest against being controlled, attempting to self-regulate, or not having ample freedom). If the behavior was perceived as another language, we may approach it very differently.

Throughout the book, you will find a number of examples and stories, identifying perhaps new ways to look at behavior. We have built BEHCA in a way that will help both the person needing extra support as well as those supporting them.

BEHCA is similar to the Fitbit, a high-tech tool that offers a stepping point for making change. The big picture goal involves behavior change and promoting health and fitness, just as BEHCA promotes recognition of influences, reflection, and shifting of perspectives (#SeeBeyondBehavior).

The Passion Behind It All

As someone who experienced a high level of trauma throughout my childhood, working with children was perhaps inevitable. My career has continually evolved, allowing me to both heal my own journey as well as support those I encounter along the way. So often we fall into a career path that is directly related to our passion and I believe this allows us to heal in a way that typical therapies may not offer.

My personal experience both in the stressful and challenging times as well as working through it has provided opportunity for me to shift my lens and gain new perspectives. With the evolution of me, I have been able to put into practice a trauma-informed approach, less due to education, rather my own experience and knowing what it is like to be sensitive, have swirling thoughts that won't go away, and feelings of isolation or that I would never fit in.

I believe most often we underestimate what is truly going on within a person and we show up with our own limitations, preventing us from seeing the whole person. My behavior throughout my childhood was all over the place and assumptions were made about my intellect, attention, and ability to function.

As I have grown and gained a strong foundation, I have realized there is much more to the outward expression, therefore asking questions are my common place. In other words, no one asked me - they made statements, based on assumptions. To their credit, that is what we are taught to do, and I was not exactly offering up a lot of information. Then again, no one tried.

In my career I have asked mountains of questions, because that is what tells another person you want to hear and see them. If we are meant to help another human being, we must first let go of our own agenda, schools of thought, teachings from our graduate cohort, or any other canned approach. Let it go and open up to the idea that there is far more the child or person in front of you can teach you by asking questions than any book will ever provide.

My education and certifications are perhaps impressive in some way, while my experience and education from those I have supported through the years is beyond articulation or gold.

Each and every being I have worked with has taught me. When I thought I had it all figured out, I fell on my face and quickly realized, no - I am still learning and will never stop. Because each of us is uniquely different and we all have our own story. The similarities and correlations are fun, but that is only a small part.

The journey each of us travels is worth learning as this is the handbook to human behavior and decoding the language of behavior itself. My hope is to offer my thoughts and insights gleaned from these experiences in a way that also challenges how we currently show up as professionals and adults supporting those who need more assistance. We are never too old to learn.

Pen-and-Paper Beginnings

As a special education teacher, I found myself trying to track data via pen and paper, to later download into a fancy, yet not very intuitive, Excel sheet. Even with the low-tech version, I was pretty darn proud of what I accomplished once all the data had been uploaded. A telling graph as proof of outside influences on behavior caught people's attention. Parents, colleagues, and administrators were impressed with the visual display (graphs) that I had painstakingly and manually compiled, showing connections among absences, changes in schedule, disruptions, and behavior (specific to decline in behaviors).

My work continued to evolve over the years in ways that would become a little more efficient and useful, but all of the systems still involved pen, paper, and manual data entry for several students, requiring a lot of time. My search for a better way was tireless, while it typically led me to one dead end after another. Data collection was the way to prove where a behavior was coming from and if the strategies were in fact working or not; yet there seemed to be this key component missing how to effectively and efficiently track data to uncover patterns.

Over two decades later, as a behavior consultant, I found the same problem to be true, but even more so. I was constantly trying to figure out ways to convince parents to track food, behaviors, seizures, environmental reactions, sibling interactions, and so much more in a daily log. This daunting task I was requesting seemed impossible. I was consistently met with glossed-over eyes, which were silently screaming that I was insane to ask them to do one more thing. But I needed this. We all needed this data.

Data drives appropriate goals and proves if we are implementing the strategies correctly, while further identifying areas we might be missing.

The request was coming from a place of need for evidence to support our next steps, and without the documentation, we would continue circling the same conversation: how do we stop this undesirable behavior? Asking parents to track what I wanted was never going to happen, no matter how cool or willing they might be, but my knowledge and experience told me the need for data was nonnegotiable. How could I satisfy us all?

Imagining an App

In 2013, this conversation came up with my co-founder, Michael Krol, who founded a company (Germinate) specializing in application and software development. Taking full advantage of this connection, I pressed my idea to build an application until he, too, could see the usefulness of such a tool. Over a period of months, we dialogued, went back and forth, established a basic foundation and made preparations to move forward in building the app. At some point, we both began to see this could work. We collaborated with software developers, educators, speech and language pathologists, occupational therapists, psychologists, state and county case managers, other behavior consultants, and parents. All the collaboration pointed in the direction indicating we were on the right track from the behavioral perspective, as well as the development viewpoint, and the need was there.

As life has an incredible way of creating detours, we went on a bit of a side journey for a couple of years. Life also has a way of turning detours into useful course changes. Our move to Puerto Rico from Portland, Oregon, would end up becoming a catalyst for the development of BEHCA, while also offering another perspective into the world of human behavior. Being in a different culture with entirely new experiences and parenting expectations offered opportunity for new perspectives.

During our travels, we became very close with another family. They shared with us an experience they had been through with one of their children, which led to further discussion about BEHCA. Their story solidified the usefulness of BEHCA in the world of not only disabilities but parenting in general. After hearing their story, we thought BEHCA could have influenced some of the interactions and supports and lessened the duration of the struggling behavior of their daughter. Data insights could have provided a quicker view into what was going on, with more clarity. As it was, this family struggled with supporting their daughter for nearly three years before they realized the *purpose* of her behavior.

Upon discovering the setting events and triggers for the behavior, the family was surprised while also relieved there was an explanation and a place to move forward from. I have asked permission to share this story, and the names, locations, and specific details have been changed to protect the confidentiality of the family. First, I want to share a general example of what I mean by **setting events** and **triggers**.

Setting Events - Example: *Imagine you wake up to a loud, crashing sound coming from your kitchen. As you jump to your feet, you step on a sharp pencil. In pain and frustration, you hobble to the kitchen to see your cat had simply knocked over a bottle of water. There was nothing to clean or pick up other than the bottle, so you stumble back into bed. Unfortunately, your heart is now pounding, your foot aches, and you cannot go back to sleep. It is only 4:00 a.m., and you do not usually wake up until 6:30a.m. Even more aggravated, you toss and turn for the next two hours, finally falling asleep thirty minutes before your alarm goes off and you are startled once again. You angrily get out of bed and jump in the shower, only to now realize you have a report due at 8:00 a.m. you had forgotten about.*

As you rush like crazy to get ready, you forget your lunch on the counter and drip yogurt on your shirt on your way out the door. As you sit in extra heavy traffic, you begin to stress about this report you had forgotten about, and you get a little distracted thinking about the subject of the report and do not notice the person with their blinker on next to you. The person impatiently swerves in front of you, nearly hitting you.

You slam on the horn, yelling, swearing, and outraged at the nerve of some chump to cut you off.

This is not how you normally would respond; in fact, you rarely, if ever, swear or honk your horn. Due to all the events that took place, your patience and resilience were down, and your overall stress was up, limiting your attention. Specifically missing the person who was trying to change lanes. This story outlines an example of <u>setting events</u> and how they impact our daily life.

Triggers - Example: *Further outlining the aforementioned story, the <u>trigger</u> in that scenario is the person swerving and cutting you off. This might otherwise be called the last straw of multiple events adding up, resulting in challenging behavior. Either way a trigger is the event that occurs right before the dysregulation or frustration. But the event alone is not responsible, only the final one.*

George and Amanda's Family

George and Amanda met via an online dating site. George had previously been married with two children, Violet (age six) and Fred (age four), while Amanda had also been previously married with two children, Roger (age seven) and Samantha (age ten).

The first time all of the kids met, they hit it off in a way that was incredible. They seemed to be connected as if they had been brothers and sisters all along.

George's wife had passed from cancer a year previous to his meeting Amanda. Amanda had been divorced for nearly six years and was the primary parent to her two children. As time continued on, they merged into one household. They were incredibly mindful of how both Violet and Fred might feel, blending the family with a new brother and sister.

Both George and Amanda talked extensively with one another, often including friends, family, and the children. They held family meetings to talk about how everyone was feeling abundant new things were happening and to offer opportunities to clear the air, if needed. They did their best to support all four kids, while also recognizing there would be ups and downs given the circumstances. They remained open and flexible.

After about a year of living as one family, there seemed to be some notable behaviors with Violet: refusing to eat, shutting down (not talking), and acting aggressive toward Roger at times. She and Roger were very close, yet she would lash out at him the most: scratching, kicking, or throwing things at him. Roger was very quiet and reserved, so his reaction was to just get out of the way.

When Violet and her brother Fred would get together, they would laugh out of control and lose awareness of their bodies, eventually hitting and kicking each other repeatedly, all the while continuing to laugh; this would normally result in some kind of furniture being knocked over or something breaking. Violet was older, but she would often look younger in these moments, from a behavioral perspective.

The out-of-control behavior was not always present; in fact, it seemed to come at strange times. Amanda had a background in psychology and education, so she was watching closely, but she wasn't seeing any clear indicators of what might be triggering these behaviors.

After a few years, the couple decided to make a big move. This meant they would be far away from friends and family. They thought of this as an adventure and an opportunity to connect more individually, as a close family. They worked with a counselor before and after the move, to help with the transition.

Nearly a year had passed since the move, and Violet's behaviors appeared to be going away entirely. Then during a visit to their hometown, they noticed an immediate regression and a spike in her overall anxiety. This introduced a whole new perspective as well as revealed influencers. Amanda had some knowledge of tracking behaviors, and she understood the psychology of trauma, grief, and the development of the brain.

They had been visiting with friends and family, primarily on George's side, and those individuals were all directly linked to George's late wife, so it made sense there would be this stressful connection for Violet. Amanda and George talked about how simply being back in their hometown may have added to Violet's stress (setting event), as it would bring back strong memories and emotions. The family members and friends who had been in her life from the time she was born added another layer of emotions.

Through her behavior, Violet seemed to return to the age she was when her mom passed, about age five, even though by now she was nearly ten. This is common with children who experience loss and is a part of the grief cycle for kids. In one way, this behavior was totally appropriate, while in another way, Violet had developed some unhealthy expressions to add to the regression. She was not eating, and she would completely shut down unless she was hyper-aroused and flinging her body in every direction, laughing and screaming.

George and Amanda decided it was time to sit down and talk with Violet. They were able to ask her how her body was feeling, what she noticed upon returning home as well as seeing all the friends and family. After several conversations in which George and Amanda would ask questions, they were able to gain some really important insight. Violet expressed feeling other people's sadness about her mom not being there, and that was really hard for her to feel, and maybe this affected her body. She also was able to link her shutting-down behaviors to being reminded of what happened and her own sadness from missing her mom.

She was not able to connect the pieces with the behaviors or why; however, considering she was so young, she was well on her way to becoming a reflective human being. George and Amanda assured her that nothing was wrong with her and her reactions were normal, and they were hopeful that over time, instead of displaying the undesired behaviors, she might ask to talk or get support when she had those feelings.

The one area in life Violet could control was her food intake. Unfortunately, her body type is very thin, so this continued to be a place of concern for both George and Amanda. They often worried her pattern would develop into a long-term habit, hard to break as she entered into puberty and societal pressures potentially exacerbating any concerns.

More visits from family and academic pressures continued to contribute negatively. Violet was really controlling her portions (eating only a few bites and insisting she was no longer hungry, even with preferred foods), and Amanda, who had grown close with Violet, decided it was time to get help. First, she tried one more time to talk with her individually.

As they began to discuss what had been observed and all the previous conversations as well as the progress that had been made, Violet started to cry. She said she knew she was withholding food from herself, but she did not understand why. She expressed her desire to be skinny, as that made her feel good, but also knew this was not healthy. As they continued to talk about her emotions and all that was going on internally, Amanda asked her, "Are you missing your mom as you are starting to grow up and do all these things she should have been here for?"

Violet fell forward and burst into tears. She said yes and sat with Amanda for a long period, crying and letting her sadness escape. Amanda assured her this was very much okay. As they ended their conversation, Violet gave Amanda a hug and said, "Thank you for the conversation. I needed it."

Later that day, Violet again thanked Amanda. Amanda and George noticed her eating a lot more at dinner, which was a good sign. And she has continued for some time now to eat healthy portions.

How BEHCA Could Have Helped

While this story seems to have a happy ending, there are some points that should be noted: First, this entire story took place over five years, and the guessing that occurred in those years was beyond measure. The family still keeps a close eye on Violet and her eating, as it can become dangerous to her health quickly.

If this family would have had access to BEHCA, they could have been tracking the outside influences, changes in schedules, people coming and going, as well as Violet's behavior. They may have recognized the pattern within the first year, very clearly, and been able to address this with their counselor. Instead they guessed, jumped around, tried a variety of strategies, assumed what the cause without evidence was, and overall played a game of process of elimination.

While this strategy worked out for this family, in a less equipped home, the outcome may have resulted in a more dramatic scenario. Violet's family was reflective and observant, well versed, educated, and experienced in being able to interact with such an intense concern. In most situations, this could have escalated to hospitalization and/or psychological evaluations.

Violet and her family were fortunate to have the opportunities they had and the ability to dialogue through the difficult life transitions. This example is important to note, as it presents minimal complications; free of disabilities, Violet is verbally articulate, and her cognitive ability allowed for extended conversations. Even with the limited complications, the process of finding ways to support Violet was challenging and frustrating at times.

Added deficits or lagging skills, only further complicates the investigation and discovery of underlying influences. This story illustrates the complexity of human behavior, emphasizing how important observation beyond behavior is. The behavior itself, rarely tells us its truth; rather, the environment and variables surrounding the behavior have the details, and with these we can put together patterns in which we can begin to build a complete story.

Having data that tracks behavior congruently with environment and health-related influences allows us to identify the trends quicker. Data also allows us to eliminate possibilities a lot faster, gaining insight into the setting events and triggers. Have a tool that also looked at all the interventions would have provided clear feedback to what was helpful or ineffective.

Language of Professionals

In a sea of acronyms, we need to speak in a common language and ensure we are recognizing all humans need validation and respect.

Language is a primary way we are connected and has a huge impact on how we feel about one another. When we feel as though we are understood, as well as understand to whom we are talking, the level of trust and willingness to compromise, collaborate, and make decisions increase. When we do not feel good about communication, tension takes hold, and nothing good comes for either side as an unintended power struggle often occurs.

Sometimes as professionals we create a subset of language that only our colleagues and those working close to our field understand. This exclusivity is not intentional, but to others, such as parents, it can feel like a power move or perhaps that we are speaking in code. While I can appreciate that perspective, I have come to realize that usually we have absolutely no idea we are doing it, because the language comes with time, habit, and naturalization to our environment and those we speak with most often.

I can recall starting out in the educational field at the age of nineteen, frequently overwhelmed with the topics of discussion. The first couple of years continued to feel as if I were absorbing an entirely new language. I was learning new acronyms and abbreviations, how to write reports from a factual basis, rather than emotional, dialoguing with both the student and staff following a crisis cycle, and developing a deeper understanding of the social and emotional component, influencing a student's capacity to learn or focus.

Around the third or fourth year, I felt more comfortable with what I heard, how to interpret it, as well as how to speak in the same language as my fellow colleagues. Continuing forward in my career, I realized each subgroup had their own way of speaking, interpreting, and assessing. Those in educational services districts, public schools (general and special education), in-home services, mental health services, and universities all spoke a certain way. Most often they are similar, if not the same, languages; however, the way in which people go about presenting information can make the languages appear completely unrelated.

Each subgroup has commonalities however; their basis in understanding comes from different philosophies or theories, different enough that each has formed its own subset of language. As we continue to read or study specific areas, we develop a more concrete language around each subject. While this is part of educating ourselves in a specific field, we unintentionally isolate or exclude those we are supporting by speaking what I might refer to as a foreign language. Obviously, it is not literally a foreign language — rather a subset, of language that is foreign to those outside of the specific professional field.

I will continue to refer to foreign language in this context to validate what those we are supporting may feel. This chapter is extremely important for a few reasons: to identify the first breakdown in communication between those offering services within a system and those directly supporting the individual; to validate the fear of those walking into meetings or needing to receive services yet not knowing the language to speak to get the appropriate supports; and finally, to examine how each of us sees and/or interprets behavior.

BEHCA was built with the intention of building bridges between systems providing services and breaking down the barriers in communication.

Breakdown in Communication

When communication becomes tense or difficult, we lose perspective of the purpose of the conversation or task of a team. When communication becomes compromised in any way, our quality of living decreases significantly, as stress takes over our ability to navigate effectively.

When a situation includes multiple perspectives (e.g., those of education, in-home services, mental health, advocate, and parent/guardian), communication becomes a significant trigger point in the breakdown of relationships between school and home, home and providers, county/state services and home, county/state services and school services, and so on. The commonality in all situations is the difference in language and perspective based upon how a certain behavior is presented. A neutral investigation from all parties involved creates an opportunity for each person to express their valuable input, while ensuring the collaboration remains as open as possible.

This is important to note, as BEHCA is encouraged to be utilized in all environments to be optimal. Having clear, open communication specific to those we are mutually supporting is critical to the success of increasing that person's quality of life in all environments. BEHCA offers a less subjective way to communicate, decreasing the opportunity for misinterpretation or increasing tensions.

BEHCA is able to do this by simply tracking the hard evidence and events of the day with only a small section for notes. Each person supporting an individual has access to the application, so everyone also has shared access to all that has happened within that day and an understanding of any potential setting events that have influenced the individual's behavior up to that point. Again, this is an excellent tool to begin to decrease difficult communication among environments.

While BEHCA is an application specific to collecting and analyzing data, it has the function to become a virtual communication among multiple environments.

This component alone allows a decrease in stress, due to the language being common and mutually understood and the data being tracked as evidence-based rather than subjective observations typically written in communication logs.

Validation of Fear, Frustration, and Stress

Parents, guardians, and support providers can become easily frustrated, fearful to ask for assistance, and/or stressed due to their perceived inability to articulate accurately for the particular audience. If you have traveled to another country or tried to communicate with someone outside of your native language, you may know the stress of being unable to communicate clearly or be understood.

A similar example is you sitting in on a doctoral lecture and being called on to answer a question when you have absolutely no knowledge of the subject area. Both scenarios could result in multiple responses; all of them may include a level of fear (not knowing or understanding the language/material), stress (elevated heart rate, flush skin, short, rapid breathing, and other symptoms), or complete shutdown (letting whatever happens happen and not attempting to clarify or understand).

Being aware of the potential (most likely, inevitable) communication breakdown in meetings or with practitioners allows us to become more mindful and ask for clarification when we do not understand, or it begins to feel like tension is building. Most often, tension can be remedied with further questions, clarifying the desired outcome or expectation, as well as understanding why this may not be met, as requested. BEHCA is a powerful tool to both articulate common language while also illustrating evidence for or against specific supports, strategies, or interventions, leveling the playing field through positive supports.

Example: A school meeting with a family who has requested supports for their son, Jacob. He is in the second grade, struggling to meet benchmarks in math and writing as well as exhibiting aggressive and disruptive behaviors. The team has met a few times to review current academic and behavioral concerns. The parents have asked for support, as they are unclear of what to do.

Recently, the family was able to gain a confirmed diagnosis of ADHD from a brief parent assessment provided and later reviewed by the doctor. The school team was able to begin the initial eligibility evaluation process, given the parent request and the historical data with both academic deficits and behavioral challenges. Over a course of two to three months the school completed a series of assessments, evaluations, observations, and daily data collection to support their overall determination of eligibility.

At the first meeting following the evaluation process, the specialists interpret their reports based upon the work they completed with Jacob. Below are the fictitious and briefly summarized reports by the variety of specialists.

General education teacher: She knows Jacob the best out of the team so far, as she has had Jacob in class for nearly eight months now and has had the most communication with the parents.

Speech and language pathologist: She was the one who conducted an evaluation of Jacob's speech, as there were some concerns with his articulation. She also did a secondary assessment for the autism spectrum disorder (ASD), to be reviewed as the communication portion of the ASD evaluation.

School psychologist: He proctored both an academic and IQ assessment, distributed a behavioral rating scale evaluation (including both parent and classroom teacher reporting), and completed a few observations.

Special education case manager: She completed a brief interview with Jacob along with an observation during one of his more difficult transition periods (lunch to handwriting class). Her role has been very minimal, and she does not know Jacob very well, having met him only a week before this meeting.

School vice principal: He is present in a supervisory role as well as to help with any accommodations or placement decisions.

Autism specialist: She has completed a few observations, done an evaluation directly with Jacob, and interviewed the parents in collaboration with the school psychologist.

This meeting has eight participants, including the parents. The family has never met the specialists, but they may have received mail, emails, or phone calls from them throughout the process. The family is very nervous, unaware of the process outside of what was briefly discussed with them when they signed consent to evaluate a few months earlier. Leading up to this meeting, the parents have felt very unsure and unclear as to what to expect.

To begin the meeting, the special education case manager lists all the reports they will be summarizing and then jumps to introductions of those at the meeting. As the team quickly introduces themselves, the parents are beginning to feel their hearts race, and their heads are feeling a little cloudy because they are not completely clear with who everyone is, nor do they understand a lot of the language (acronyms and testing names) the specialists are using. To avoid looking stupid, they just sit and listen, not asking for clarification even during times they clearly do not understand.

The school psychologist begins to review his reports and starts throwing terms out like *coexistence*, *autism spectrum disorder*, *anxiety*, *emotional regulation*, and *sensory processing disorder*. The psychologist, unaware of the growing anxiety of the parents, continues to read his report until the father interrupts him. The parents latched on to one term they have heard before and fear. The father asks, "What are you saying? Is our son on the autism spectrum?"

The autism specialist quickly jumps in and tries to explain. As the determination has to be a team decision, she is concerned about the psychologist speaking too soon and the whole team not having had a chance to hear all that was found. Unintentionally, the autism specialist forgets to reassure the parents and, in the process, shuts down their ability to ask further questions. Instead, she redirects the psychologist to carry on with his summary, while saying their question will be answered at the end of the meeting.

The specialists continue to review their summaries, using more language the parents have never heard. The parents are particularly frustrated because they see themselves as educated and normally understanding information given to them. The father is a chemist and has two different graduate degrees, and the mother is a biochemical engineer. They are beginning to feel more frustrated with the process that is unfolding and how they seem to be falling further behind in all that is being discussed.

Jacob's mom finally interrupts. "Look, I just want to know: does my son have autism? I feel like we entered into a room with a bunch of people who are more interested in looking at their reports than talking to us, his parents, about what is going on with our son."

A little stunned, the autism specialist tries to assure them they will answer their questions. She reminds the parents that the team has not made the decision, and they are close to discussing that portion. Again, frustrated with this response, the mom elevates her volume and demands answers.

The vice principal steps in at this point and lets the parents know this is the process they are supposed to follow and that they are about to discuss the determination right now. Even though this process has been explained to the parents previously, as well as in this meeting, it just does not make sense to them. Do these professionals not talk before the meeting? From a parent's perspective, this all seems disconnected and confusing.

At the same time, the school does have protocols to follow, and while the team is more than likely already in agreement with a potential determination, this cannot be discussed until all reports have been reviewed and the team has a consensus of the evaluation conclusions, including parental input, and, finally, has determined eligibility for special education services.

Having compassion for the parents and what they are going through is underestimated among education professional at times. In addition, being mindful of what we are telling parents along with interpreting the reports in a way that would make sense to others outside of the educational world are incredibly important steps. The language of educational processes is difficult to navigate unless you are someone who has spent a good amount of time in the system. We cannot expect parents and/or guardians to understand all that we are talking about.

The meeting ends shortly after the team, along with the parents, determines Jacob is eligible for special education services under the code of *autism spectrum disorder*. The parents are in shock. They had heard this briefly from their physician but had not really given it a lot of weight. They could see the reports were clearly showing their son qualified in all four categories, but they had not prepared for this part. This meeting went so long the team has to reconvene to develop an IEP (individual educational plan) for Jacob and determine placement.

In their minds, these parents were given terrible news about their son. Autism is lifelong and comes with a lot of added stresses. Now they need to go home and process not only what just happened in that meeting but what this means for their family.

BEHCA, in this example, could have provided a daily dialogue, updates, and interaction with the data collection. With BEHCA, the parents would have been more involved in providing details of what Jacob's day looked like outside of school (his daily eating, overall health, supplements, sleep, screen time, and behaviors at home). Having a communication tool like this allows the parents a sense of empowerment within the process, from the beginning. The collected information from both home and school would have further validated any findings from the assessment process as well while providing a platform for both home and school to walk through the process more collaboratively.

As Jacob interacted with the various specialists, his parents would have gained firsthand knowledge of the day and time he went. This would have given them further context within the meeting and eased their overall anxiety. Opportunities to hear and be aware of what is happening throughout the evaluation process could establish a solid *bridge* between school and home that lasts throughout the child's academic career. This small, initial investment may return a profit far greater than we realize.

How Each of Us Interprets Behavior

If I could highlight one section of this book for everyone to read, potentially twice, this would be it. *The staggering difference in how each of us sees or interprets behavior is based upon our personal experience, values, and potential knowledge base.* The goal in this section is not to identify who is wrong or right, rather, to note the differences and how significant the communication will be among all of those who are tracking the behaviors and understand the importance the description of the behavior is.

Example: Johnny is an eight-year-old boy who has been reported as aggressive toward his family and frequently hits his siblings and mom.

Mom: "Johnny is constantly hitting his siblings."

Sister: "My brother cannot control his body, and he is flailing into me all the time."

Brother: "Johnny is so annoying because he hits me every time he sees me, but I do not understand why because he does not seem to be angry."

Dad: "Johnny really struggles with keeping his hands to himself and is constantly hitting those around him."

Behavior consultant: "From my observation, Johnny is struggling with his spatial awareness due to his proprioceptive functions. What that means is Johnny is experiencing his world through a lot of stimulation [touching or hitting things]. He is not aware of how hard it may be due to his underwhelmed sensory [takes a lot for his body to feel it]. Furthermore, in my observation, he is never upset, rather, attempting to interact with his siblings who then became annoyed, agitated, or angry with him for what appears to them as hitting."

Clearly, in this example, the majority of the family reports Johnny as an aggressive child who frequently hits, whereas the behavior consultant has a vastly different perspective. None are wrong or right, simply offering different perspectives based on knowledge and experiences. The behavior consultant is able to offer new insight for the entire family to digest and begin to shift perspective, they need to adjust their own responses due to the new information that Johnny is not doing this on purpose and is not aware of how hard he is hitting.

How to track this in BEHCA

Pre-Crisis Behavior

- *sensory-seeking with hands or arms* (this would not be *hitting*, as this is a different behavior all together)

There are two ways to consider Johnny's behavior: he is lacking spatial awareness (is not aware of where his body is in relation to the environment around him), and/or he is seeking input by slamming his body/arms into solid objects or people. Johnny is not intentionally trying to hurt or hit anyone. Some of this behavior may be from seeking attention (a way to communication or engage), whereas the other portion is seeking sensory input (wanting to feel his arms and body).

If this were tracked as sensory seeking, there might be notes indicating a hypothesis written in the notes section as to which form of engaging the contact was initiating. This further requires support providers and/or parents to be mindful of his actions and watch carefully to what he is attempting to communicate or gain. The closer the reflection, the more apparent the differences become.

BEHCA collects the data, while it also requires us, as support providers, to step back and take note beyond the collection of data.

If we begin to see Johnny as a child expansively experiencing his world through sensory seeking, rather than a child out of control who hits, we come closer to understanding the world he experiences. As we begin to notice the subtle differences in his movements, we gain a closer look into his form of communication. Decoding the idiosyncratic behaviors Johnny provides insight to begin putting in place strategies to support progression towards replacement behaviors. Having longer collection of data also allows us to see behavioral patterns that later can be put into a plan to "prepare" for knowing upcoming transitions or events where Johnny might struggle more.

Intervention Strategies

- *Communication cards*
- *Devices*
- *Supports*
- *Yes/No cards*

Self-Reporting

BEHCA also features a section where the individual can self-report their tolerance scale (what they can handle from green to red), an emotional status, digestion, and screen time). The access panel can be opened on their own device under their own sign-on. This allows the data to be saved in comparison to the other data collected.

This information also allows the individual to gain a sense of empowerment within their skill-building. This section is customizable as well and will continually be updated to reflect emotional regulation skill building. The goal with this section is to add autonomy to the process of understanding another person's world.

Self-reporting can be viewed side-by-side to the data collected, giving us further insight. While this information is helpful, it can ultimately be a tool to begin teaching strategies and encouraging interaction with the emotional reporting as well as where they are on the tolerance scale. This feature allows BEHCA to fall under the category of assistive technology as it is both supporting the provider as well as the individual in developing skills.

This section can be turned off, given the individual is not at a place to participate or interact. The recommendation is to explain the application, allow them to have access, and attempt to have them be involved on some level with the reporting. Different sections can be activated, while other sections may not be relevant at that time.

EMOTIONS

Tap or click to enable or disable emotions you would like this individual to track.

ENABLE TRACKING OPTIONS

Select which data points you would like to allow this individual to track on their own. Please note that data they enter in these fields can overwrite data you enter in the same fields.

 DIGESTION   SCREEN TIME

 SLEEP HOURS   WATER INTAKE

 WEIGHT   NOTES

Example: Sally is an eleven-year-old girl who has been reported by both teacher and parents as disruptive, unfocused, and disrespectful.

Teacher: "Sally is very loud in my class and will intentionally blurt out answers without raising her hand or being called on. This is extremely disruptive to the class and her peers."

Mom: "Yes, Sally does this at home sometimes too when her dad and I are having conversations. She listens to our conversations and will interrupt with her input, which is not appropriate. We are sorry, but we do not know how to correct this behavior, and it seems to be getting worse."

Dad: "Sally is extremely disrespectful and interrupts conversations constantly. We have tried to take things away from her, talk to her about how this makes others feel, give her incentives to go a period of time without interrupting, yet nothing seems to work."

Behavior consultant: "Perhaps Sally struggles with impulsivity, which is linked to her ADHD that she has been diagnosed with. During the observation, it was clear that after she blurted out her answers in class, she felt bad, yet it seemed her body was not allowing her to stop before she spoke."

In BEHCA, you would track this as *interruption* or *impulsive interaction*. The strategies you might use are asking Sally to count before she says something or having a visual reminder to raise her hand and count to ten before she says anything. These strategies would be tracked in BEHCA as working or not, which would then be excellent evidence for a doctor, behavior consultant, or any other specialist working wspecific strategies.

Pre-Crisis Behavior

- *impulsive interaction*

Intervention Strategies

- *verbal prompt with visual support*

Reflecting on what her purpose is in blurting out allows those supporting her to gain insight into her experiences. Is the behavior purposeful, meant to be disrespectful or annoying, or is her filter not as developed as her peer's? The more we identify a child as having a behavioral problem, specifically, challenging one, the more they feel disappointed in themselves, and a lack of confidence continues to grow, further exasperating the behavior.

We, as parents/guardians, providers, and educators, want to offer supports while also changing our language and understanding around the behaviors. Our behavior changes by gaining new lenses to view the individual with. Shifting the e enough, the individual does not feel inadequate or burdensome; rather, they begin to understand more about themselves, in a positive way.

Example: Anthony is diagnosed with autism and has a coexisting seizure disorder. He is now being reported as aggressive toward staff and requires a two-to-one staff ratio for his safety, as well as the safety of others. A meeting has been called to review his IEP.

The special education teacher introduces the concerns and begins describing the behavior: "We have been experiencing two to three episodes a day where Anthony will start hitting staff for what appears to be no reason. He just starts swinging his fists, and if we are sitting in close proximity of him, we are getting hit. The staff have tried a variety of interventions, including giving him his favorite sensory toys and taking him for more walks outside, but the episodes seem to be increasing, although the behavior only seems to last for approximately five to ten minutes and then subsides."

Mom: "Have you noticed him having seizures?"

Teacher: "No, we have not noticed any seizures lately. We keep a close eye on those for sure."

Mom: "Well, in the initial evaluation [a couple years previous] we discussed Anthony having what are often referred to as silent seizures, and he has them daily—that we observe at home—which nearly always results in him lashing out with what might appear to be aggression. This behavior is an involuntary control of his limbs, as a result of the seizure. He will appear to be confused and mildly agitated and often will swing his arms in what might seem like a hitting motion. Then, he will calm within five to ten minutes."

Teacher: "Oh, wow, maybe we need to be observing this more closely. I will go back and read the original report for a refresher, but I also think we need to do some careful observation to see if we notice any warning signs that will allow us to get out of his proximity."

Mom: "Yes, this would be good. I can tell you our observations have been that he will stare for thirty seconds to a full minute just before he takes a swing, and his eyes will close kind of tight with a slight head jerk back."

Teacher: "This is really great information. We had no idea to be looking for this, and it makes so much sense, because Anthony is not an aggressive boy."

Mom: "I am concerned he is having these episodes more frequently. We should be watching the food he is eating along with other environmental influences. Perhaps you could keep track of this too?"

Teacher: "Yes, we would be happy to track that."

In this scenario, the parent is the one who has the actual language to interpret the child's behavior that was present. The school team quickly learns the behavior is in fact an involuntary response to a seizure, not aggression. If the parent had not been so aware and articulate with her observations, this scenario may have resulted in more restrictive settings for this young man because the staff was under the impression, he was doing this on purpose.

No matter the situation, having BEHCA on board with Johnny's team, offers a substantial input, as Anthony also has complex communication needs (he does not verbally communicate). Breaking his behaviors down into the categories might look like:

Health Challenges

- *Seizure* (in the health section)

Pre-Crisis Behavior

- *Involuntary body movement following a seizure* (with added notes at the bottom of what was observed before, during, and after. The reason we would categorize the involuntary body movement as a "pre-crisis behavior" is because this is most often reacted to as a "crisis or dysregulated" behavior, yet it is not and should be addressed as a support with the understanding he has most likely had a seizure.

Challenging Behavior

- *Increased physical aggression* (this would be if we missed the pre-crisis and were not able to offer or support with a strategy. This behavior just gets documented and supported in the clear and concise way Johnny needs support in a crisis, no interventions applied at this point.)

Implementing notes on the *health* page in *tracking foods, sleep, digestion,* and *weather*, would be important as they are influencers of both seizure activity and his behavior. This will allow support providers to identify any, clear, triggers related to the onset or increase of seizures.

Anthony experiences a world where his brain is being jolted or rebooted, involuntarily, throughout his day. The physiological aspect of this experience results in a loss of learned behavior, communication, and ability to regulate. When seizures are present with any person, this kind of perspective must be primary when attempting to decode complex behavior within their world. They are attempting to navigate unchartered territory without GPS, a map, or gained cognition to use other skills, every time they have a seizure. Experiencing this must feel incredibly isolating, confusing, and frustrating.

Sometimes we overlook these aspects, as the behavior itself tends to be so intense. Recognizing the behaviors are, in fact, challenging, we must also acknowledge the complexity and challenging part of being that person, first. We have the GPS, maps, and cognition; therefore, we need to fill in as we learn where the gaps begin. BEHCA provides a map to identify the cracks or areas in which we need to build put a road map, with back up detours.

Application of Knowledge Gained

During one of my busiest years of behavior consultation in Oregon, I decided to take on the task of training an intern. During this time, I had 3 candidates' interview, trial a week or so and ultimately come to me and say how difficult this particular career path was. In different ways, each of them expressed how much I may underestimate my deep knowledge and how easy I make the job look.

Surprised, and feeling a little defeated that I might not find anyone up for the task, I interviewed one more person, whom I had met while working with a family. She was bright, courageous, and full of energy. She had expressed interest in finishing her master's in speech and language pathology and loved working with kids. She had been working with a family we were both providing services for and had recently started working as an assistant in a specialized classroom.

She could not have been more perfect; however, I knew she was young, and after my recent experiences, I was nervous about her potential. I offered for her to come interview and discuss the opportunity for an internship. She accepted with eagerness to get to work. As the weeks flew by, we both worked side-by-side on cases, dialoguing, challenging one another on perspectives, and ultimately dissecting the various situations. She would often talk about how much she was learning and how excited she was.

Approximately three months had passed when she came into the office one morning excited to share a story about her weekend. Her invigorating energy captured me as she went on and on about how she had used the strategies I had been teaching her. Self-reflection and observation skills had entered into a pivotal point with her fiancé and family over the weekend.

She was delighted in letting me know how successful it had been and how well it worked when you just *shift perspectives*. A smile began to spread across my face as I realized this young lady had not only been learning a new career path - she was implementing much of this new knowledge into her personal life, showing a higher level of understanding. Of course, I could not have been prouder in that moment.

This story outlines the foundational methodology of BEHCA and how using such a tool can transform how we look at our entire life. We all have behavior that can be shifted as well as understood in different contexts. This book and BEHCA will be as effective in those willing to step back and observe their own behavior and influences, as it will be for those we support. We have to be willing to adjust, make compromises, and shift our perspectives to become optimally effective in increasing the quality of life of those with challenging or difficult behavior.

While it is not required to be an expert, it is recommended to be open to changing ourselves before we attempt to influence change in others.

How Schools Use BEHCA

Writing and Developing IEP (Individual Educational Plan) Goals

An IEP is a document developed within a team following an eligibility determination (from the school) that a child needs extra support based on a federally identified (coded) disability. This document is legally required to be reviewed once a year, however, more revisions can be made throughout the year upon parent request or a team's determination. The team also determines goals for the child, and based on those goals, services and placement are established. The document is also federally governed and protected based on IDEA (Individuals with Disabilities Act).

Using a data-tracking application from school-to-home exponentially increases the effectiveness of collaboration and goal implementation. Even without the home-to-school component, the tracking specifically linked to behaviors to show progress or lack of progress in specific areas is powerful in IEP meetings. The IEP team is intended to collaborate and determine supports, interventions, and placements based upon the data.

BEHCA provides another level of assessment in recording how individuals respond to their environments. BEHCA also promotes a Positive Behavior Intervention System approach (PBIS), always. This is an excellent tool for identifying increased sensory-seeking and what interventions and tools are the most successful. The team then has viable evidence for or against purchasing particular tools for classrooms.

IEPs are often written and tracked with subjective observations. This practice is what states a goal as having been met or not. This has served a purpose and still qualifies as data-driven; however, having hard evidence in addition to analyzing the behavior-to-influences deepens the impact and ultimately improves the plan with solid tracking and collection, as well as increases understanding of what the person being supported needs. This also allows us to further provide a more individualized plan, promoting a higher quality of life.

Before an IEP is written, the use of BEHCA can be implemented to create an initial overview or support the movement from a 504 to an IEP or prove that the 504 is sufficient as is. Having data with analytic capabilities increases the integrity of the eligibility process while also providing substantiated evidence supporting proposed levels of supports. This data also keeps us focused and observing in areas we might not otherwise have noticed. The data also supports team decisions, reducing stressful and tense meetings between home and school. When evidence is provided through daily data and graphs, there is very little room to argue; therefore, all parties are seeing and speaking the same language through the view of what the *data has presented*.

Tracking the data becomes extremely easy in comparison to current structures that still require lengthy data entry, often involving paper and pen, as well as further individual analyzing of minimal inputs. BEHCA creates a real-time opportunity to track all aspects of an individual being supported and to gather as much information as possible to increase quality of life and experience.

Creating Solid, Data-Driven BSPs and FAs

As mentioned previously, data collection with BEHCA substantially adds integrity to our goals and increases the effectiveness of the goals. The behavior support plans (BSPs) and functional assessments (FAs) would clearly state what the data/analytics found, and a variety of suggested ways to provide interventions or supports around the discovered information, would be shown to be effective or ineffective. Eventually, this collection of data would provide a timeline of where the person being supported started and if there has been an increase or decrease of specific behavior based upon the use of given interventions and/or supports.

Example: Rowan will be transitioning into middle school, and the school team would like to create a transition plan as well as review current goals. Three months remain before the end of the school year. There are enough school days to gather six weeks of data and hold a meeting. The school determines having as much information as possible is imperative, so they invite parents to use BEHCA during this period of time at home.

Home input and data strengthen any goals or supports suggested and agreed upon, as it is a whole child the team looks at rather than one behavior that child is expressing, in one environment or setting. With a whole view into the child's day, the team begins to see more patterns and influences, and more impactful problem-solving can take place. Parents also begin to feel they too have a part in this process, allowing them to become more involved as well as understand the process from a different perspective.

The team eventually convenes with all data and begins to discuss the findings. The evidence shows Rowan has more self-injurious behaviors (hitting head with hands and banging head on solid objects) on days the barometric pressure drops below 30"; the behavior significantly decreases when the pressure rises above 30". This is very interesting and new information for the team. Perhaps some of this information needs to be shared with the physician, occupational therapist, or any other specialist who could help with further interventions.

With this particular scenario, one meeting alone cannot fully determine a complete solution. But Rowan's team does know something they did not previously and can provide a variety of supports and inform all the individuals working with him, as well as be more observant of barometric pressures. The team can also be prepared to have soft objects readily available and possibly provide more pressure for him, as this may support him on those specific days. There may be additional suggestions from doctors or practitioners that the school and home can implement as well.

The data also shows an increase of seizure activity when Rowan has several portions of sugary and high-carbohydrate foods. Obviously, the school cannot change Rowan's diet, but this could be a discussion between home and school. Perhaps Rowan is sent with a lunch from home and avoids sweet treats. The school could also be sure to avoid treat access and redirect Rowan when he is at lunch, if necessary. Again, the physicians may have additional information on this as well, especially with the data showing the trends.

His team also notices that when he has two or more seizures in a day, the following day Rowan is less willing to comply with instruction or routine. Data shows an increase in agitation. His pacing and rocking is also elevated, according to the trends. The team speculates the seizures are causing him to regress or go through a period where his ability to process is impacted.

He might also be physically tired, creating another agitation that he is being asked to work. Based upon this information, the team discusses supports and has a secondary schedule for Rowan on the days following multiple seizures, where he is doing less processing and more basic, routine tasks, to limit his frustration. The team may also build in more sensory and relaxation time (audio books, music, drawing, or whatever interests Rowan has) to avoid power struggles or frustration on his part.

Having a concrete piece of data in front of the team means less guesswork and more direction, reducing stress of both parents and school staff. The goals also include interventions based upon what the data is showing, therefore allowing the team to come back and look directly at the results rather than saying, "Well, we have noticed Rowan is doing better with his self-injurious behaviors, so it looks like he has mostly met his goal."

Often, this information is based upon more recent interactions, not so much on long-term yearly information and patterns. BEHCA provides this information with long-term evidence for teams to continually dissect, looking for new patterns or correlations.

> *My observation has also been that we see cycles of behavior, making the less concrete collection of data, primarily based on more recent findings, less accurate. In other words, Rowan might have two, maybe even three, months with minimal seizures and behaviors. While this looks amazing and might happen just before the IEP review, the accuracy of those three months being the new normal is unclear. Perhaps the three months he is less likely to have those behaviors is in the spring, when he has access to the outside more often, his food is different, and the barometric pressures are not fluctuating as much, but he then goes into another cycle of declining behavior following this two- or three-month period. As BEHCA collects data over time, his team begins to see these cycles. This is extremely powerful information that could offer a lot of answers in a current system where we are not always finding the exact solutions.*

Providing Resources for RTI

Another area where BEHCA is incredibly useful is with response to intervention (RTI), which is put in place before specialized instruction or accommodations are considered for a 504 plan. Some schools in the United States are starting to implement behavioral RTI, which is typically funded through general educational dollars. This is important to note, as the focus would then be on general education students who are showing a need for more support specific to behaviors.

When a school identifies a child with concerning behaviors, there are a few strategies in place they may follow. One of those strategies is RTI, as mentioned before. This means the school might pull the identified child out of his or her class for check-ins with a school counselor, a specific teacher, or another adult trained in RTI. The goal is to find ways to connect with the child and understand where the behavior is coming from. Once this is identified, the staff works with the child in learning new skills.

BEHCA allows school support staff to track data and collect a baseline of information that allows the interventions to become more effective. The data allows them to potentially address basic needs, supports, and interventions with minimal assessments. The tracking also provides a direction for the potential school team to address what is next for the child, given the brief interventions are not enough.

The collection of observable behavior as the child moves toward a potential 504 or IEP offers a quicker, more accurate look into the child's needs or potential supports. A school team can then determine what additional assessments are needed and if there are any interventions to implement right away. Meanwhile, BEHCA can continue tracking and providing information to the team as goals are set and met. Within the sixty-school-day assessment period, BEHCA can play a critical role in collecting information that supports or clarifies any of the assessments.

BEHCA is accessible on any computer, mobile device, or tablet; therefore, inputting data is easier and can be immediately analyzed without any additional steps. Making observations leading to the data being entered is the only work needed to gain a wealth of knowledge. This capability also allows home-to-school or other provider environments to input data, expanding the view of the child or observable person. Again, this allows the team to look at the entire individual, rather than a snapshot of their day with limited understanding of what might be influencing him or her.

Using such a tool for RTI validates the efforts of RTI as well. Through data, we show the supports and strategies are effectively intervening with the noted behavior. With RTI, the need for communication from home-to-school would perhaps not be necessary. However, if the interventions lead to a more conclusive decision toward special education supports, this tool is suddenly a place that both parents/guardians and school support staff can see a common ground and collaborate, reducing tension and miscommunication that often happens without intention.

Communication In All Environments

As mentioned before, BEHCA can be used as a communication tool from one environment to another for a variety of providers within various settings. This is one of my favorite parts of this application. As we were sketching out the initial structure and uses, I got really excited when it became clear this could be utilized in all settings and viewed by all support people. How cool is that! Perhaps I am excited because I see so many perspectives from home-to-school and other environments, and one of the biggest complaints is the lack of communication or the kind of communication from home-to-school and school-to-home. Both sides express almost the exact same things, only from very different perspectives.

Both school and home are including emotional — and opinion-based information that is more often misunderstood than embraced, leading to huge conflicts and tensions. BEHCA takes the subjective nature out of the back-and-forth communication. On each daily entry panel there are places to add notes, so messages can still be conveyed, yet the school cannot stop at writing, "Jolesca had a good day". Teachers and others must also enter data. The parent actually sees what the day looked like in terms of trackable information. And the school sees data from home too, rather than only "Rider is feeling grumpy this morning, and he pushed his sister."

> *The tension that can culminate among attorneys, advocates, and angry parents or staff is reduced significantly because the entire team is seeing the same data, at the same time. The team meetings are more efficient due to parents no longer waiting to see the collection of data; rather, they are actively participating in collecting the same data. Both parties show up already knowing what the trends are and ready to discuss them, decreasing long reports with needed explanations of language and justified reasons for proposed interventions.*

Of course, some of this is still going to be present; however, both the parents and the school staff knowing what is going to be discussed in the meeting before they arrive quickly reduces one of the most common areas of tension. As an advocate, I have found this area to be one of the most significant contributors to tensions building and clashes transpiring.

The other area is language and lack of explanation and/or understanding. Given the use of BEHCA, the parents are informed, experiencing the tracking and beginning to see the patterns that schools already are looking at and speaking about. The parents feel empowered and involved, rather than feeling like wall art in a meeting with a bunch of people telling them what is going to happen with their child, with only bits and pieces making any sense.

> *Having been in the roles of parent, teacher, advocate, behavior consultant, and observer, officially and unofficially, my partner and I built BEHCA to be a data-driven collaborator and potential peace-bringer. As an advocate, my heart hurts when I see individuals working toward the same thing but getting hung up on language, interpretations, opinions, and/or conflicting personalities. All of these things cannot be eliminated, as we are human, after all; however, we can certainly do better about inclusivity of our process and how we come to the table to collaborate. BEHCA is a beautiful tool to assist in such a partnership.*

The empowerment of parents also brings a level of collaboration to the meetings, which is what I believe all of us ultimately want. Through this application, a level of communication can occur, providing a common ground to move forward. The school also begins to see the incredibly valuable information the parents have. I have witnessed more often than not that the school staff speaks to parents as if they know better than them, even when they are not really meaning to.

Another observation: often communication within the meetings happens from a place of assumption on both the parent side as well as the school side. These assumptions come from lack of knowledge, understanding, and awareness of the other side. With BEHCA, the assumptions do not go away entirely. However, it provides a view into the other side's world as well as a clear indication that both sides are truly doing what is best for the child or adult needing support.

Individual Families and Care Providers

Similar to how BEHCA helps schools, the application provides a more conclusive and data-driven look into what is happening throughout the day at home. Families and care providers are often overwhelmed with interventions, supports, ideas, and therapies. I hear many questions like "How do we know if any of it is really working or doing what it is claimed to do?" "How do we know those interventions or supports are not actually contributing to some other behavior, due to physical or emotional responses to any number of interventions?"

When a person has complex communication needs, we do not know with certainty these answers. We can guess, we can assume and get really close, but sometimes we miss big clues because of our own agendas. Or we simply get so involved with the immediate situation that we do not see the outer influences or little things having impact on the daily routine or responses to such influencers.

When setting up a customized profile in BEHCA, a bit of consideration is needed. This is an opportunity to begin hypothesizing what might make sense or exploring thoughts you may have had but never had opportunity to clarify or prove. BEHCA allows you to track in a way that offers a more qualified and supported answer to your questions.

This being said, we as parents and care providers need to be ready to see and accept what is found. This might mean that discovering the therapy that just required your family to take out a second mortgage is actually not the best. Perhaps this means adding things you had not considered before or thought to be less impactful.

BEHCA can provide a great deal of insight, and parents and teachers need to be prepared for that, along with being open to reflect and be ready to make adjustments when the data shows changes might be needed in the way of food, environmental inputs, or other areas that require other people in the home to be impacted. Sometimes this adjustment by others in the home can be as difficult as dealing with the behavior being displayed. Therefore, these areas should be carefully noted and weighed to determine what brings a more sustainable, healthy environment for all people in a home.

Of course, the information is only information without any implementation of supports or interventions. The application could simply be a device that tracks and communicates from one environment to the next and allows behavior consultants and the school team to set goals and make suggestions. However, in the event a person wants to fully optimize the use of such a tool with the assistance of the school staff, providers, behavior consultants, and other practitioners working with the observable person, the success could exponentially increase.

While my dream is to provide an optimal outcome for all families and care providers, I recognize beginning with something that feels more objective than subjective is an acceptable start. It is an opportunity to collaborate in a way that has not been done previously with schools or vocational programs and other support providers. Through this collaboration, areas will be uncovered and discovered. Looking at this kind of data may create an opportunity for those serving this community to come together in a way not known previously. BEHCA is only a tool; how the information is used is entirely up to the those inputting and analyzing the data.

As someone who has poured my heart and soul into this work for years, I love BEHCA because it provides so much potential while it also teaches observation and reflection. I also see the application being a long-overdue tool for tracking and communicating from home-to-school.

Here's an example of how BEHCA might be used at home:

Example: Shalise has moments where she becomes overwhelmed with a physical response, resulting in her thrusting herself backward and onto the floor. She continues to thrust backward, often resulting in severe bruising if not immediately protected with a soft intervention. When individuals get close to her, this behavior increases, and she tries to grab and scratch at the person. The family has tried a number of supports and interventions. They do not always know when the episode is going to happen, as it seems unpredictable and without a clear trigger.

The family has worked with a number of behavior consultants, and the school has implemented a plan to physically assist Shalise to a soft place to allow her to work through this process in a safe place. These episodes persist for approximately thirty to forty minutes, sometimes an hour or more, at least three times per week. The environment does not seem to matter. She has experienced these episodes in school, in the community, and at home.

The family has guessed environmental noise might have something to do with it. Sirens seem to agitate Shalise, and if they are long and in close proximity, this almost always results in an episode. Fire drills at school frequently result in an episode. The family has been puzzled, however, because there are times the noises do not seem to impact Shalise in this way. The family has noted that when the weather changes drastically and the noise is added, there might be some impact, but they are not certain, and because of their seemingly incomplete hypothesis, they have given up on guessing.

In this situation, the BEHCA profile would be very specific to include *thrusting* and *dropping to the ground* behaviors, and utilize the comparisons with *environmental* impacts, including but not limited to barometric pressure, rain, and temperature. In addition to those types of *environmental* impacts, which are automatically tracked based on location within BEHCA, we would add in sirens, loud alarms, or other noises. Perhaps we would add a closer look at dietary intake along with *digestion* (constipation, diarrhea, or normal) correlations.

Desired Behavior

- *Increased use of communication device*
- *Responded to communication device after 1 prompt.*

Pre-Crisis Behavior

- *Grunting*
- *Clenched fists*
- *Furrowed brow*

Challenging Behavior

- *Thrusting*
- *Dropping to the ground*

Intervention Strategies

- *Provided 3 sensory choices*
- *Intentional distraction*

- *Go for a walk*

A specific profile that allows us to track specialized areas and outcomes helps us to further develop our hypothesis and determine if we are on track or completely off the mark. When we can see trends over more than sixty days of collection, we can evaluate and determine if we need to further refine our tracking. In the meantime, we continue looking and taking closer note of what is happening. When we engage in this behavior, we begin to automatically become more in tune with potential agitators or predict behavioral outcomes.

Shalise's entire family should be aware and involved with tracking data, as everyone who begins to observe offers another perspective and can see things that perhaps might be overlooked by another. Also, this practice should be employed when setting up the profile initially. For example, the siblings should be involved in the process to help give a sense of involvement and belonging to the process. Siblings can offer incredible insight, and this is an excellent area to involve their input. Plus, if they have suggested tracking a factor, they are going to be an additional set of eyes to monitor that specific area.

Sometimes siblings, those we would have otherwise thought to be nonparticipants in the process, discover the most meaningful things. The suggestion of involvement does provide a more inclusive plan, adding to sibling empowerment and sense of belonging, especially important because other children in the household often feel otherwise left out during this evaluation.

Every family has a way of going about the process, and for this reason, these are merely suggestions. This process does come with discovery that has the potential to challenge our own personal limitations. This is the reason for me indicating that families should be considerate of what the data might conclude as well as be prepared to make potential changes based upon findings.

Potential Changes and Impacts of Learning New Things from the Data

Dietary Changes: This can be incredibly difficult, depending on how well received such a change is with all members of the family. My experience is that when the child needing a dietary change is not excited about this and sees that others in the home do not have to change, progress is limited. Therefore, this should be something to carefully consider, and a strong commitment should be made before it is initiated. Starting and stopping and restarting again only exacerbates behaviors.

A friendly suggestion on this part: do not make the change unless you are ready to make an entire family change. This can be considered if the child is more open to dietary changes as a rule. I also recommend starting with only one thing at a time, not trying to remove several foods at once. Start with what everyone is able to agree on and build from there. The more the entire family can be involved with any changes, the more successful transitions will be.

Scheduling and Planning: This can be extra difficult for families who tend to be more spontaneous. Clearly, there are ways around some of this, and it depends on how much of a schedule a child requires. Perhaps the goal is more about communication or preparation for events or transitions. Some kids are going to have great difficulty with the slightest changes.

This being said, the same philosophy applies with starting where you can and building from there. The family's behavior often changes more than that of the child being observed. This is potentially the single most important part of this process. We have to be patient with ourselves, recognize behavior change takes time, and adjust along the way. Working with professionals can help with understanding and allow the process to be a bit more streamlined. There are plenty of options to learn and apply new strategies if you are willing to be flexible and go a bit out of your comfort zone.

Conversations with Doctors: As certain trends come up and show medications or supplements are not working, causing ill side effects, or in fact *are* working, we need to be able to advocate and ask questions. This can be difficult, as doctors are sometimes seemingly unapproachable when you question the regimen they have determined best for their patient. The good news is that BEHCA offers hard data, giving you tangible information to present for review.

This area is a little less difficult in the way of impacting our daily schedules, but it can certainly be difficult having the conversation(s) about making changes to medications or supplements.

Training and Informing Others: This is an important area when it comes to implementing any change within your home or an individual's daily routines. Knowing how to train someone can be difficult as well. This might be where a professional would be helpful. Otherwise, my recommendation is to look at all documentation already written for your child. Create a synopsis of what you see as the most important.

Once you have gathered this information, look at the data, trends, and patterns within BEHCA and begin to develop a list of strategies and interventions. As you are writing them, or perhaps as a behavior consultant writes them, review them verbally with people who might be working with the person being observed. Discuss the different ways each strategy would be helpful, along with ways to further implement the strategies, based upon that person's personality. The more empowerment you feel in assisting others, the more successful and effective the overall attempt to change behavior will be.

How to Most Effectively Set Up BEHCA

In previous chapters, I started to identify some areas to consider and be aware of when setting up a profile. With the following, I outline a few examples of incidents, behaviors, and potential individuals who would benefit from BEHCA. In the examples, I do my best to identify exactly how I would set up their profile, what that might look like throughout their day, and what the hypothetical data would offer to the family, school team, agency team, or other program supporting the individual.

Example: A thirty-five-year-old adult experiencing autism and seizure disorder.

Ed is currently living in an adult group home with three other gentlemen. He attends community vocational program five days a week, for five hours per day. During this time, he sweeps hallways and empties trash. Overall, Ed is quiet and keeps to himself. He enjoys drawing and spending time playing games on his iPad. Ed also enjoys opportunities to walk around the community, though this has been limited due to him easily getting lost. Plus, he is prone to seizures and needs to have another adult with him at all times.

Ed periodically becomes extremely agitated about not being able to go outside unattended. There seems to be some correlation with seizures and the days he becomes agitated (more agitation the day after a seizure). Ed can become so agitated he begins to engage in self-injurious behaviors, hitting himself in the head and banging his head on walls or the floor while screaming. The staff in his group home have tried to offer him walks with assistants, but this seems to increase his agitation even more and will often result in him increasing the intensity of his self-injury.

One might speculate his behavior is due to his desire for independence or to get away from his housemates. While this is an excellent consideration, the solution is more complicated than letting him go out on his own. There also seems to be something else going on, perhaps physiologically. To understand this further, data needs to be tracked; some strategies should be implemented and tracked as well for efficacy. To set up Ed's profile, I would do the following:

Health: All medications and supplements; daily health rating (scale of 1 to 10), including digestion (constipation, diarrhea, or normal); his diet, specifically in the area of sugars and carbohydrates; any other notable area related to Ed and his daily routines.

Environment: Weather, barometric pressure, moon phases (already tracked with BEHCA); potential sensory irritations for Ed (specific noises, lights, smells, other); schedule changes; other known antecedents/setting events/triggers; document in notes the days of seizures and any specific observation of the day before; be mindful of his moods, clarity in focus, or ability to articulate, and/or his increased sensitivities to noises, sounds, and smells.

Desirable Behavior

- *Accepting another option than a walk*
- *Going on a walk while letting staff follow at a small distance*
- *Talking with staff about concerns*

Pre-Crisis Behavior

- *Making low grunting noises*
- *Pacing*

Challenging Behavior

- *Self-injurious behavior (hitting head with hand, hitting head on solid objects)*

Intervention Strategies

- *Offer 2 sensory choices (he previously picked)*
- *Comedy/distraction*

Health Challenges: *Seizure;* Time, date, duration, and type of seizure (as recommended in BEHCA); document any injuries that may have resulted from a fall during a seizure in the notes section.

These areas should be tracked in all settings throughout Ed's day for a minimum of sixty days to ensure a solid amount of data. From this information, the team can assess any patterns and look at frequencies and intensities in relation to seizures and environmental and health influences.

Perhaps there are items that do not seem to be impacting any part of his day. These areas could be dropped. And perhaps there are some areas that seem to be showing up that are not as closely tracked or tracked at all; they now need to be added. Perhaps there is a correlation between barometric drop with increased precipitation and Ed having a seizure. From this observation, the data should be shared with his doctor, and further discussion should be had as to why this might impact him or if there needs to be any adjustments made to his current medication regimen or treatments.

Seizures can be elusive and should be carefully observed. Most often the person will have very clear indicators before a seizure, and it is extremely important to have those indicators outlined in a plan for all persons providing support. The type of seizures can change, which is equally important to track.

Seizures literally scramble the neurotransmitters in the brain. In one way, the brain is kind of going through a reboot after a seizure, which can explain the agitation, confusion, forgetfulness, exhaustion, and other out-of-character behaviors that might follow. But all of this is unique to each person; therefore, the observation, tracking, and clarity must be documented to assist in providing the highest quality of living supports possible.

Ed may be out of sorts the day after a seizure, but because he has lived in this home for so long, everyone is used to this and never notes it in his documentation. Part of this disorientating behavior, including his desire to leave the house unattended, may be related to post-seizure behavior. With this information, an agreement could be made to allow him a ten-to-fifteen-foot distance to explore. His goal might be to simply familiarize himself again with his surroundings, and a way to do this is to get outside and reconnect.

This example is one that could go in a variety of directions but offers a quick view into how BEHCA could support in the way of finding a potential influencer. With Ed being a grown adult, the idea of giving him space needs to be considered; yet his safety is also something that must be a high priority. However, sometimes our deep desire to keep him safe prevents us from seeing why he might want to get out of the house or what he might be getting from that re-entry.

It has been my experience there are times silent or absent seizures go undiagnosed due to the lack of observation and close monitoring of behaviors. This is of particular concern for those who have more complex communication needs (are not able to verbally let us know what is going on or articulate something is wrong). These seizures are quick and most often do not result in the person falling down or over. Again, my experience is the individual usually looks like they are staring off into space (hence, the *silent/absent* term).

I mention this as someone who has been in many homes and observed hundreds of children. I have witnessed some of these traits and let parents know they may want to check in with their physicians, later learning that in fact their child is experiencing partial-complex seizures throughout their day, most likely contributing to much of the difficult behaviors.

Interventions in these situations can vary. They can also become extremely complicated because every person is unique.

However, BEHCA was created with these individuals in mind, as my heart has gone out to these families so much over the years. Our hope is BEHCA will offer new insight to families and physicians for these particular individuals who experience seizure disorders.

Example: A twelve-year-old boy experiencing autism.

Carlos is an active young man with sensory-seeking behaviors that are often misunderstood as well as not redirected effectively. Recently, Carlos's school has been reporting Carlos expressing sexual behaviors, and they are concerned about his ability to be around his peers. His parents see this behavior at home but simply redirect him to his room, to which he seems to respond well. Carlos has complex communication needs and is able to verbally articulate a few requests; however, he does not have full range of verbal interactions to express his needs, wants, or desires.

The school has started isolating him more, due to the increased behavior. In response, Carlos has been scratching and hitting staff more frequently. The school has been trying to track data, but it is difficult to track everything throughout the day, and they use pen and paper, later entering the information into an Excel sheet. They are only able to track his sexual behaviors, hitting, scratching, and refusal to work at school, so the information is limited and solely focuses on the negative behavior. Strategies have been implemented, yet nothing seems to be decreasing the incidents.

A few things need to be noted: the phrase *sexual behaviors* is most often noted instead of *masturbation, touching self, hands in pants*, or *seeking-sensory response by rubbing penis on soft objects*. Suggestive general language written in permanent documents is damaging and offers a very different view into what is happening. If the child or adult were actually grabbing others in private areas, trying to kiss, or displaying aggressive sexually related behavior, this would also be considered sexual behavior.

Self-discovery and sensory-seeking, similar to what Carlos is engaging in, are merely a part of puberty that most people experience, yet they are not closely observed throughout their day. It is my observation that limited explanation about body changes are offered to individuals with complex communication or intellectual disabilities. Perhaps this is due to the belief that they do not understand, because of their disability. When we are tracking such behavior, we need to be incredibly diligent in noting the difference between sensory-seeking behaviors and sexual behavior.

With Carlos, I would set up a profile as follows:

Health: All medications and supplements to be tracked daily; daily health (scale of 1 to 10), including digestion (constipation, diarrhea, or normal); sleep; any other notable area related to Carlos and his daily routines.

Environment: Weather, barometric pressure, moon phases (already tracked with BEHCA); potential sensory irritations for Carlos (specific noises, lights, smells, other); soft objects; pictures, videos, or noticeable triggers before he begins to sensory-seek or masturbate.

Desired Behavior

- *Responded to "go to bathroom" by second prompt*
- *Responded to "hands up" by second prompt*

- *Successfully accessed other sensory engagement, following redirect*

Pre-Crisis Behavior

- *Hands in pants*
- *Rubbing self or on things*

Challenging Behavior

- *Self-stimulation with hands down pants*
- *Pulling pants down*

Intervention Strategies

- *Compression shorts*
- *Increased sensory diet/choices*
- *Social stories with body awareness*
- *Utilized PECS* (picture exchange communication system)

If we wanted to track the hitting/scratching later, we could do so after the self-stimulation has been addressed. It is important to be focused on one specific behavior at a time to ensure our direction and attention on the specific behavior. Plus, we might find that one behavior is related to another, and by addressing one, the other automatically subsides.

If the compression shorts, tried as an intervention strategy, do not make a difference, and the data begins to show a correlation between Carlos's sleep and increased sensory-seeking, perhaps a regimen around sleep and sensory input can be added. Note any strategies throughout the time data is being collected to indicate the effectiveness. Looking at multiple influencers (environment, screen time, interactions, certain times of day) here will also allow us to see more clearly the sensory types and impacts of environmental factors on his increased sensory-seeking.

On each of the pages, there is a General Notes section for additional information. In this situation, notes should be added with any strategies being used. For example, with this particular area, compression shorts and shirts are extremely effective because they provide pressure, which offers sensory input and decreases stimulation (the penis is no longer moving around as freely). If this strategy or another is being used, it should be noted.

Example: A ten-year-old girl experiencing cerebral palsy.

Miryam has recently started showing signs of physical aggression (scratching, throwing head back, and biting) during bath time and feeding time, specifically during dinner. Her routine has been the same, with very little change, since age four. Her mom has always been her primary care provider. Her dad does assist at times but rarely during bath time. Recently, her school routine has changed, and her mom learned that Miryam has become more confined to her wheelchair throughout her school day.

Mom is concerned about her being in the chair way too often, and this might be a contributing factor to Miryam's behavior. Her mom had a hard time convincing the school to see this or acknowledge it was a contributing factor. She has asked them to give her more floor time and offer her the walker more frequently to get from one activity to another. The school responded by letting Mom know that Miryam has become more difficult to transfer from the floor to her chair, so it is safer for her remain in the chair.

The concerns from parents are: Miryam is not being given freedom to explore and is potentially getting frustrated, as well as her body may be getting sores from being strapped into a chair all day. Her nervous system also seems to be a little more sensitive lately. Mom has noticed her agitation over clothes (getting hot and cold at unlikely times in unlikely situations). Again, her mom tried to talk to the school, but they do not seem to be hearing her concerns.

Her bathing times have become dangerous for both mom and Miryam, as Miryam is almost as tall as her mom and weighs nearly eighty-five pounds. She is very strong and will throw her head back repeatedly and scratch mom, as well as try to bite her. She will laugh when she is engaging in this behavior but does not stop when redirected. Recently, Miryam threw herself back when her mom was transferring her into her seat in the bathtub, and her mom fell, dropping Miryam on the side of the tub and hurting her back, while Miryam laughed and laughed.

Mom wonders if her laughter is actually an anxious laugh, because it is different than her other laugh, and this laugh has only been present more recently, particularly around these times when she is physically aggressive. Mom was able to get assistance from the state to help with the bathing routines, but Miryam is still showing similar behavior with the care provider.

Her dinner routine has also involved throwing food and spitting it out when being fed. She becomes more upset when the food is removed after this behavior, but she seems to continue the same thing at the beginning of each meal. Mealtime is the only time she has to be back in her wheelchair, as this is where her tray is. This allows her to reduce aspiration and gives support during her meal. Mom has considered getting another kind of supported chair for the table, rather than her wheelchair; unfortunately, it is expensive.

School has also reported more scratching, biting, and throwing her head back during toileting routines or any transitions from floor time. They also report similar behaviors with the eating routines. The school has asked Miryam's mom if anything has changed at home, while Mom has pressed the school about letting Miryam out of her wheelchair more often as well as letting her interact with general education peers more frequently, like she had been doing the year before.

The teacher is new and feels that she can provide Miryam's educational needs within the specialized classroom, therefore limiting her access to the general education setting more than the previous year. This was not due to any behavioral concerns at first, but Miryam's behavior has become more aggressive at home and school, following all of the changes. Miryam will ask to play with friends, but she has not been given opportunities within the last few months.

Here is how I would set up BEHCA for Miryam:

Health: All medication and supplements to be tracked daily; daily health (scale of 1 to 10), including digestion (constipation, diarrhea, or normal); sleep; bath times (describe each event in the notes section); specific notes of any red spots on her body from sitting in her wheelchair too long each day, morning and night.

Environment: Weather, barometric pressure, moon phases (already tracked with BEHCA); how many hours she is in her wheelchair; how many hours she is outside or doing exercises (floor, walker, physical therapy, occupational therapy, other).

Desired Behavior

- *Engaged in conversation with peer*
- *Used communication device to request or answer question*
- *Requested to play with peer*

Pre-Crisis Behavior

- *Fidgeting*
- *Increased noises*

Challenging Behavior

- *Physical aggression*
- *Strange laughing*

Intervention Strategies

- *More time out of her chair*
- *Communication device offered*
- *Staff modeled use of communication device*

The goal of this process is to increase her use of the communication device and reward her every step of the way. As she responds (in a positive way), promoting more positive behavior; this means encouraging the communication, even if she is disliking or protesting. Specifically looking for the times she initiates the desired communication, which is an indication she is learning the functioning as well as the cause and effect of its use.

In this particular situation, a potential hypothesis may be about Miryam being in her wheelchair too often and having limited interaction with peers, resulting in her increased behavior. While this is an excellent place to begin, her ability to communicate (using her device appropriately and having people respond with what she is requesting) and gain freedom with this is potentially a contributing factor. She is a ten-year-old and protesting is a part of this age. Especially given the prepuberty weight, her hormones could also be playing a part (maybe would explain her being hot and cold in unlikely situations). The other area of concern is the new staff and new schedule, and perhaps her needs are being overlooked at school unintentionally.

In this example, it would be imperative to gather data from both environments for at least sixty days, with a review after thirty of those sixty days. During the review, both school and home should collaborate on putting together some ideas for interventions, including changes in schedule and overall approach to Miryam daily living. They both need to be open to whatever the data is showing and know that once the interventions are in place, the data becomes evidence for effectiveness of the proposed changes.

After thirty days, if the interventions are not making an impact, the team needs to continue to look deeper. BEHCA might offer strong evidence showing weekends with extremely low reporting of behavior, due to her being in her wheelchair only for outside walks, while the remaining time is on the floor or in her walker. She also does not seem to have as many incidents involving eating on the weekends, leading the adults to further conclude the wheelchair is a definite factor.

With the brief data, I would present the evidence to the school along with some suggestions of activities that have worked in the past, while also including the OT (occupational therapy) and PT (physical therapy) specialists at the meeting for further ideas within the school setting. I would also encourage the school to have her interact with her peers when she does need to be in her wheelchair, so there is less resistance and feeling of frustration.

Furthermore, I would also express concern around her communication requests being ignored. The goal is always to encourage as much dialogue as possible, but if we are constantly not following through or telling her no, then it will feel like she is trapped and even more limited with her freedom. Her complex communication needs do not imply her lack of intelligence, and this needs to be stated frequently and consistently reinforced.

All of these areas would be supported by the data shown from home-to-school. Perhaps other outside influences are noted as having some influence, and these areas should be considered as well as discussed in regard to potential supports or interventions, specifically because they could play a part in future behaviors and the information will become valuable.

Conclusion

BEHCA will begin to change the way we look at behavior and collaborate with families, and most importantly, it will allow an opportunity to come together as a community. The most successful organizations have been found to be excellent collaborators with the community and fellow professionals within the field of work. This is not a reinvention of the wheel, but a reevaluation of its design.

As parents, Michael and I hope our collaboration and dedication to creating BEHCA brings a sense of clarity and empowerment to understand at a deeper level what all the professionals are always talking about. We also hope this tool, in the hands of parents, allows them to become certified as the experts they already are, even when not credited as such. Empowerment goes a long way!

As a behavior consultant, I hope this brings a sense of grounding information to the field of behavior expertise. We always seem to be trying to figure out ways to navigate, collect, and understand outside of our time with an individual. The goal with BEHCA is to provide a new level of accountability to the professional world of writing plans and assessments based upon more concrete data. BEHCA also aligns philosophical value with trauma informed practices, PBIS (positive behavior intervention systems), collaborative problem solving, and restorative justice, making the tool even more powerful as a way to teach and train.

As a teacher, I can visualize how BEHCA will offer a window of opportunity to change the way we approach and see the individual child, communicate with the family and care providers, and offer incredible new insight, without added work. The initial idea for this application arrived when I was still teaching, so the idea of educators using this is really exciting! I also see the power of what can happen when all parties are participating in the process of tracking, observing, and then collaborating on the findings.

As an advocate, I have shed many tears over lives affected by behaviors and missed opportunities in data collection and analysis. I see so many potentials this application can bring, if there is open-mindedness and willingness to collaborate. In the testing phase, school staff were jumping out of their seats with excitement at how this could help not only tracking but also communication. An example of this was when I was in an IEP meeting (2017), advocating for a family and child, and had reviewed what the family and I had set up on BEHCA. Not only were there several excited questions from the individuals in the meeting, they all individually asked to speak to me following the meeting.

In another meeting, with a director of special education for a local Oregon school, there was excitement about the idea of analyzing and comparing data rather than simply collecting, as the other programs have done. The conversation was extensive about the way the communication with families would also decrease current climates with meetings. One of the biggest struggles is the amount of time, money, and staff resources that are spent on difficult meetings, most often made difficult by a breakdown in communication.

All of these perspectives are so much fun to witness, and we look forward to seeing what BEHCA can do for you! We would love to hear your success stories or suggestions for future improvements at feedback@behca.com.

Several parents have told us that because of these strategies, they no longer focus on directly on decreasing or lessening the behaviors; rather they had changed their perspective of the behaviors and were responding to them differently. This kind of feedback shows exactly the purpose of BEHCA. We hope to help decode the behavior and recognize it as a language rather than a challenge, and through different lenses we learn more about the individual.

Together we can see beyond behavior!

Glossary of Terms

Accommodations: Supports; no material can be modified or removed; the person must maintain the same level of expectation as developing peers, while having extra supports around him or her. This is unlike a modification, in which curriculum can be changed to scaffold for the level of understanding.

Anxiety Disorder: three potential areas: *Generalized anxiety disorder*; display excessive anxiety or worry for long periods of time and face several anxiety-related symptoms. *Panic disorder;* recurrent, unexpected panic attacks, resulting in sudden periods of intense fear that may include palpitations, pounding heart, or accelerated heart rate; sweating; trembling or shaking; sensations of shortness of breath, smother, or chocking; and feeling of impending doom. *Social anxiety*: ("social phobia") a marked fear of social interactions or performance situations inducing a feeling of.

Autism Spectrum Disorder: Autism spectrum disorder (ASD) is a neurodevelopmental disorder that impairs a person's ability to communicate and/or interact with others. This disorder may include repetitive behaviors, interests, and activities. These behaviors can create significant impairment in social, occupational, and other areas of functioning.

Autism spectrum disorder is now defined by the American Psychiatric Association's Diagnosis and Statistical Manual of Mental Disorders (DSM-5) as a single disorder that includes disorders that were previously considered separate — autism, Asperger's syndrome, childhood disintegrative disorder, and pervasive developmental disorder not otherwise specified.

Coded disabilities: The federal codes given to states for funding and census, involving the IEP process and eligibility determination.

Eligibility Determination: The process in which schools go through to determine an eligibility code (labeled disability that is recognized within the federal data base). This then determines the level of supports and basic understanding of a child. This process is the first part of becoming eligible for special education services.

Emotional Regulation: The ability to regulate ones emotions within a variety of contexts. This regulation is driven by the brains capacity to make sense of what is happening and adjust to the environment or circumstance. The executive functioning (frontal lobe: problem solving and rational thinking) is primarily responsible for the emotional regulation.

Functional Assessment: An assessment that determines the function of behavior(s). This process may include several types of testing, observations, historical review and interviews with those who know the person being assessed.

504 Plan: A plan developed to ensure that a child who has a disability identified under the law and is attending an elementary or secondary educational institution, receives accommodations that will ensure their academic success and access to the learning environment.

Individual Educational Plan (IEP): A collaborative document developed to ensure that a child who has been found eligible to receive services, due to a disability, identified under the law, and is attending an elementary or secondary educational institution receiving *specialized instruction and related services*.

Positive Behavior Support Plan: A person-centered plan that is followed by a Functional Assessment. This plan includes a list of strategies and interventions that will assist in supporting an increase of desired behaviors, replacing the undesirable. Typically this plan would be considered a living document, that is reviewed after a collection of data to determine the efficacy of each strategy.

Specialized Instruction and Related Services: Added services (speech and language, occupational therapy, emotional regulation), and this area also includes modification to material or exclusion of particular material based upon assessments and the individual's present levels. This comes from *IDEA*...

IDEA: The Individuals with Disabilities Education Act; a four-part piece of American legislation that ensures students with a disability are provided with free and appropriate public education (FAPE) that is tailored to their individual needs. IDEA was previously known as the Education for All

Handicapped Children Act (EHA) from 1975 to 1990. In 1990, the United States Congress reauthorized EHA and changed the title to IDEA (Public Law No. 94-142). Overall, the goal of IDEA is to provide children with disabilities the same opportunity for education as those students who do not have a disability.

The four parts of IDEA: Part A covers the general provisions of the law. Part B covers assistance for education of all children with disabilities. Part C covers infants and toddlers with disabilities, which includes children from birth to age three. And Part D is the national support programs administered at the federal level. Each part of the law has remained largely the same since the original enactment in 1975

Occupational Therapy: Pertaining to a vocation or source of livelihood related to movement, proprioception, sensory seeking and other related motor skill development.

Proprioceptive: The ability to know where your body is in relation to the space around it (body awareness). These senses come from the body's connective tissues, joints, and muscles.

This sense is activated with movement, heavy pushing or pulling, and any other maneuvering that may occur within the body's structure, stimulating joint receptors.

Response to Intervention (RTI): A multi-tier approach to the early identification and strategy implementation of students with learning and behavioral needs. The RTI process incorporates high-quality instruction and universal screening of all children in the general education classroom.

Seizure Disorders: Characterized by episodes of uncontrolled electrical activity in the brain (seizures). Seizures can be hereditary, caused by birth defects, or environmental hazards. Seizures can be more common with patients who have other neurological disorders, psychiatric conditions, or immune-system problems.

Sensory Processing Disorder: A condition in which the brain has trouble receiving and responding to information that comes in through sensory stimuli (things within the environment around you).

Sensory Seeking Behavior: This is behavior that looks like the individual just cannot get enough of whatever it is they are doing. This could be related to eating, touching, spinning, jumping, mouth noises, ticks, or other repetitive behavior. A helpful tool to review can be found on http://spdlife.org/symptoms/sensory-seeking.html where there are further descriptions and examples.

Setting Events: Something that is considered part of a building foundation of what usually results in an undesirable behavior. A few examples of setting events: change in schedule, not being able to eat breakfast, increased noise in a car, lights flickering or buzzing, loud background noise, scratchy material in clothing, or not being able to have your favorite drink.

Speech and Language Pathologist: Work to prevent, assess, diagnose, and treat speech, language, social communication, cognitive-communication, and swallowing disorders in children and adults.

Trigger: The final straw or the *antecedent*. Examples of this; any of the above setting events could actually be a trigger depending on how many setting events were building to that point. You could also have very clear "triggers," such as telling a person "no." Smells can trigger reactions/behaviors, change in adult care providers, or being too close in proximity.

Vestibular System: Relating to a vestibule, particularly that of the inner ear, or more generally to the sense of balance. Otherwise more simply referred to as the equilibrium.

Questionnaire for Setting Up BEHCA

Questions to consider when developing the customization portion of BEHCA are below. If you have current plans (IEP's, BSP's, 504's, person-centered plans, or other documentation that has determined what is challenging and what works versus does not work), use those documents to align both the language as well as the tracking. Even if at first you are not collaboration with others or inviting anyone to track data. This documentation (specifically language) can often help us stay focused, speak similarly and begin to form a baseline perspective.

What is your goal for tracking the specific behavior? What insight are you hoping to gain? (this will help you identify both language as well as "what" to track):

_____

_____

How does this behavior impact the individual's life and those around them? (this will help you determine the positive behaviors that you want to see more of)

_____

_____

What are successful strategies that have worked in the past or are currently being used, and what did the behavior look like? (This will help identify positive behaviors or responses we want to increase. Think of interactions or reaction you want to see more. This will become the "positive" behavior portion):

_____

_____

How does the environment impact the individual? (This can be anything from smells, textures, sounds, particular people, places, or things. Try to be observant and creative with this section and make room for changes with the first couple of weeks, as you may begin to see more areas impacting them):

_____

_____

_____

Can you think of ways the above behavior could be redirected? (This will help you identify a variety of strategies to start keeping notes in response to the effectiveness):

_____

_____

_____

_____

_____

_____

List their *least* favorite activities, foods, people, transitions, and things they most often refuse to do (this will be used within the environment section of BEHCA):

_____

_____

_____

_____

_____

Based on the gathered information, begin to create his or her profile. Identify the areas within the environment that might become setting events (things that build up) or automatic triggers (final straw). This may be something you have to wait to add and become more observable of his or her environmental responses. As noted, lights, noises, smells, changes of weather, and so forth can all contribute to setting events.

Then set up the behaviors that you want to keep track of. The recommendation here is to set up one to four at a time. More than four becomes difficult to track and look at, while one is most optimal for really identifying a specific behavior.

Once you have these areas identified with the team or people involved ensure everyone is on the same page with language, understanding what the behavior being documented looks like in a variety of settings. Daily tracking is a must for the connections to be identifiable. The first month might be a month to simply observe the brief information known, with the intention of growing this through direct and specific observations.

Examples of what the customized section might look like:

Desirable Behaviors

Identify all positive behaviors you would like to see more of and add those into the positive behavior section. This might look like the following:

- Things they currently do well.
- Include interests/strengths that may lead to added strengths (improvements).
- Combine what they do well (have buy-in) with what we want them to shift in terms of challenging behavior.

Example: Johnny frequently hits to get attention; however, he loves interacting with others while putting puzzles together or playing games. Example desirable behaviors could be:

- *Engaged socially with soft touch*
- *Calmly interacted with peer*
- *Respectfully engaged with taking turns*
- *Clearly stated needs using words*

Pre-Crisis Behaviors

Identify all behaviors that indicate frustration or beginning emotional dysregulation, or other warning signs that eventually lead to more challenging behaviors. Examples:

- *Pacing*
- *Furrowed brow*
- *Increased pace of talking*
- *Increased volume*
- *Excessive repeated questions*

Challenging (Crisis) Behaviors

Identify up to four behaviors (try to keep it under four to bring validity to the tracking as well as less complexity). List those behaviors in the Challenging Behaviors section as general incidents. This might look like the following:

- *Physical Aggression* (hitting, kicking, scratching, biting, throwing things, pulling hair, pushing, etc.)
- *Sensory-seeking/stimming* (spinning, making noises, flapping, repeated phrases, rocking, etc.)
- *Verbally aggressive/threats* (screaming, making idle or real threats, swearing, making negative comments towards others, saying explicit phrases, etc.)
- *Self-injurious behaviors (SIB)* (banging head, biting hand, punching head/face/body, throwing body against floor or wall, slamming self-back, etc.)

- *Suicidal ideation/threats/attempts* (making threats to harm or kill self, making advances in harming self or stating preparedness to kill self, screaming "I want to die," or other variations of such.)
- *Property destruction* (kicking walls, throwing items to break them, ripping items apart, using weapons/sharp things to destroy furniture, etc.)

Intervention Strategies

Detail any intervention strategies for the individual that are known to promote positive behavior and avoid an escalation to challenging behavior. This may include strategies from the following documents:

- Behavior Support Plan goals
- IEP goals or accommodations
- 504 plan accommodations
- Trauma-informed practices

Examples:

- *Collaborative problem solving*
- *Sensory break (3 choices)*
- *Visual schedule*
- *Verbal prompt*

- *Check for understanding*

Environment

Think creatively and observe closely: the goal is to pay attention to ALL influencing variables on a person ability to self-regulate. The more agitating events, the less patience we have:

- *Particular noises* (alarms, fans, sirens, birds, dogs barking, siblings yelling or screaming, road noise in a car, windows down in a car, etc.)
- *Sensory stimuli response* (other people touching them or hugs, hair being brushed or washed or otherwise, certain clothing, tags, material, seams, etc, wind, car rides (particularly long or curvy), food (textures and flavors), showering (wet, cold/hot, soap, towels, etc.))
- *Certain people/personalities* (power struggles, limited choice giving, gruff voice or demeanor, high pitched voice, timid, unsure how to respond or seemingly fearful, specific physical features; beard, long-hair, bald, tall, women, men, children, etc.)
- *Changes in Schedule* (canceled appointments, time changes, having to wait long periods (appointment late),

new provider, new teacher or para professional, different location for school, work, or other, favorite choices no longer being available or being limited)

- *Pollen Count/Change in Seasons* (pollen is something we are planning to track regularly, in the meantime we are noticing big effects with the increased count for individuals who struggle with inflammation.)

Health Challenges: Identify any chronic or recurring health issues, like *seizure* or *migraine headache*.

Medications and supplements: this section is mostly fill-in: however, it is important to make notes of any observable influencers or changes, related to the health section. This might be particularly important when experiencing medication changes or rapid changes in specific health-related concerns; rapid weight gain or loss, increased anxiety or obsessive-compulsive disorder (OCD). *(NOTE: if your plan supports MAR (Medication Administration Records) and you have this option enabled, you will not see the basic medications and supplements in this section as they are replaced by MAR tracking)*.

Month One Check In

1. What is working well? What is not working well?

   _____
   _____
   _____
   _____
   _____

2. Are you noticing any trends or correlations between environment, health, weather, supplements/medication impacts and the behaviors? Make a simple note to review again in another 30 days.

   _____
   _____
   _____
   _____

3. Are you beginning to see patterns within the time of day or week the behaviors increase?

   _____
   _____

_____

_____

4. Does the behavior being tracked still make sense? If not, is there another way to frame or identify what you are observing?

_____

_____

_____

If the answers to 2 & 3 are no, continue documenting, however you might want to consider adding more influencing data, again, reviewing potential setting events that may not otherwise have been noticed.

If yes, continue, as you do not want to quickly assume you have it all figured out. At this point, it would be better to have 60 days rather than 30 days and ensure there are no other influencers to consider, or perhaps what you thought was causing something is not in fact it, rather a coincidence. Also, remember behaviors can come and go, and having long-term data is going to be critical in the way of developing a substantial graph with lengthy tracking.

Review current profile, check with any other individuals inputting data and spending time with the person being observed to see what their input might be (whenever possible). Make adjustments as a team and be sure to communicate if any added information was input, so everyone is on the same page.

Remember: If you change data within BEHCA, the time you have tracked starts over and your data should be considered as such. Continuing data without this note can invalidate the data. This is primarily important for agencies or schools tracking long-term goals and strategies.

What to Do With Data

Once you have started collecting data and connections seem to be clearer, you will review (optimally with everyone who is participating) the graphs and discuss what is found within the data and notes. If there are clear indicators of something influencing behavior and there seems to be some potential strategies available to help redirect the behavior in a way that increases the quality of life for the individual, begin to implement and be sure to communicate this strategy clearly with everyone involved. The key to strategies working is to be sure it is happening in every environment, consistently.

Based on the strategy, this might be something that is written into the notes pages or simply communicated and documented again later as being implemented. The most effective and accurate way to collect data, and determine if the strategy is working, would be to document every time it is used within the notes portion in whatever section applicable or simply change the behavior portion to the specific behavior needing to be shifted.

An example of this: Spencer has been tracked for aggressive behavior for 90 days and the team realized the aggression is specific to the bus transitions. His behavior increases before, during, and just after each transport (morning and afternoon). The team discussed having a support staff ride the bus to further identify what was going on, as well as track for an additional 30 days what they are observing.

During those 30 days, the support staff noted another student on the bus who would frequently screech and scream the entire bus ride. Spencer would begin banging his own head on the seat, then the window, eventually slamming his fists on the seat and himself. He would repeatedly try to unbuckle and by the time the bus reached the destination, Spencer was well into a stress cycle (in crisis). He would hit, scratch, and try to bite anyone who came over to him to unbuckle him. The bus driver had noted at one point he felt the child screaming was a contributor, however none of the team members knew just how bad it was.

Getting an entirely new bus was going to be extremely difficult, so the team had to determine other strategies. They came up with the idea to put noise canceling headphones on Spencer along with headphones for the child who was screaming, in hopes to both reduce the screaming and cancel out the intensity of sensory overload for Spencer. The team also determined they would talk with Spencer, even though he had complex communication (non-verbal), due to the observation being that he has high receptive communication and often responds to most directions.

Spencer was informed, given the headphones, and walked to the bus with the support staff on the first day of this strategy. Spencer started to show signs of distress as he left the school. His body began to sway back and forth, his head started rocking more and he was swinging his hands into himself. The staff quietly reminded Spencer he has his headphones and today was going to be a better ride. Spencer reluctantly got onto the bus, however his aggressive behavior was already less than the previous day.

Following another 30-day observation and continued strategy implementation, Spencer was reported to now be happy to get on the bus, both in the morning and afternoon. His self-injurious behavior as well as any aggression towards others had completely subsided. The other noticeable difference was the student who screamed had decreased her volume, intensity, and frequency significantly since the implementation of her own headphones and music.

In this example, the team was able to identify the potential trigger, create a plan to implement a strategy, and further observe to determine if this was effective or not. Had this strategy not been effective, the team would revisit, perhaps 15 days rather than 30.

Behaviors can often increase within the first week or two before declining. In the example above, Spencer was talked through what was going to happen and the team speculated he understood, which was why it was successful. In other scenarios this may have taken a week, if not two, to implement and finally determine the effectiveness.

Acknowledgements

This book would not have been possible without the support and encouragement of my partner, Michael Krol and his company Germinate, my editor and her everlasting patience, Kristin Thiel, our close friend and marketing strategist, Ryan Gallagher with GoodGallagher, and finally the incredible inspiration of all the courageous parents and providers I work with on a daily basis.